Shadowmouth

Vitalie and Arthur Rimbaud—scenes from life

Liliana A. Pasterska

LEAF BY LEAF

Leaf by Leaf is an imprint of Cinnamon Press.
www.cinnamonpress.com

The right of Liliana A Pasterska to be identified as author of this work has been asserted by her in accordance with the Copyright, Designs and Patent Act, 1988. © 2023, Liliana A Pasterska.

ISBN 978-1-78864-990-2

British Library Cataloguing in Publication Data. A CIP record for this book can be obtained from the British Library.

Designed and typeset in Bodoni by Cinnamon Press. Cover design by Adam Craig

Cinnamon Press is represented by Inpress Ltd.

Liliana A Pasterska was born in Poland and educated there as a paediatrician and psychiatrist. She worked in UK as a consultant psychiatrist for many years and became interested in the female condition, particularly in relation to the pioneering women writers of XIX century. Some of her poems have been published in the *Journal of the Gaskell Society* and in the anthologies of Manchester Stanza and Womanswrite groups. Her debut pamphlet was *The Third Sister Speaks* (Cinnamon Press). She is married with two adult children and three grandchildren and lives in London.

Acknowledgements

I would like to thank Jan Fortune at Cinnamon Press for her advice and encouragement.
My grateful thanks are due to Matthew Caley for all the help given during his mentorship while working on this collection.
The most special thanks go to my husband for his ever present support and interest.

Contents

Introduction	9
Prologue	11
Ancestry	12
Orphan	14
Marriage	16
Shadowmouth	17
Widow Rimbaud	19
Mother	20
Father	21
Rue Bourbon	22
Paris	24
May 1871	25
Place Vendome	27
You Happening to Me	29
Dear Paul	30
Dear Rimbaud	31
Mad at You	32
The Woman of Harare	33
Epilogue	34

for Milosz, Teodora and Nikolai, with love

Shadowmouth

Introduction

Creative genius in a rebellious uproar of adolescence—young Rimbaud defies every convention in both his writing and his life. In a soaring, cometic flight of spirit and deed, each with their strange integrity, he dismays, appals, and rushes on. He is credited with changing French poetry forever, changes that resonated through continents, and for inspiring art, thought and the way we use language for the centuries to come.

It is believed that the trajectory of Rimbaud's tragically short adult life, running so out of kilter with his youth, is embedded in the unavoidable ambivalence that must have marked his relationship with mother, the eponymous Shadowmouth, and also with his father, powerful in his absence.

The mother, Vitalie Rimbaud, grew up as an orphan from the age of five, after her mother died delivering the next baby. This life-changing event and Vitalie's employment in helping her father take care of the family and running the family farm from a young age, and a strict religious upbringing, were the formative influences on the development of her personality.

Prologue

of the African desert dunes
comes poet's roll call
hungry gusts rippling   floating
the grains under   around his ankles
caressing his feet
lifting his footsteps high   higher
Back-to-the-future poet

he contemplates poetry mayday
old ways   sentiments
gives credits   rebels   surveys
the Mount Parnassus
Graces gracing   Olympians sporting
he finds all for the taking
nit-picking will not be enough

off with their heads
all for ripping apart
no
not you   you stay
I will write to you
you always know how to say
what I want to say

the poet
verité networks surfer   irreverent believer
in resurrection by words
tweaking at the bloodline of future
nothing else will do   justice   pity
no poverty   universal experience
he seduces   invites   dares

I alone have the keys to this wild circus

To walking away from it all as well

Ancestry

i/

home
grandfather's country opus
sprawling   crouching pile
closing their long lane——-
laughter could be had there
as anywhere

the grandmother
just out of her teen years
two babes in arms
new one   a daughter
the morning rosebud

broken night   exhaustion
misty-mind danseuse
arms rounding up
soft nest closing   swaying
warm breaths mingling
milky dancing   milky loving

ii/

four years bring
looks to smiling looks
small hand to hand
fifth—ah, the fifth year
runs out of luck—
much to do with much—luck

in delivery   back-tearing pain
blood   sneaking rivulets   sly
cloudy mind snatched off
floating away   heedless
her new baby   the children
young husband

she dies
he stays on his own
some said later the daughter's
love was all he needed

Orphan

i/

some things she knows before waking
absence
to size up   take stock
vastness   to set against   wander through
sepia monotony   low flat fields
mute horizon
woods   brooks   hills to the north
stream framed in gnarly trees
watchful frogs in unruly grasses
clumps of nettles   butterflies
the cemetery

roller-skates the best name-day present
she could zoom to the grave
lie a bunch of daisies   show iPhone pictures
new pair of jeans—
dress such a nuisance in the field
back to the farmyard in a tick
wind in the blond wisps of hair
her pick-me-up

keeps coming back—
day of the First Communion
trailing white silken cloud behind her
Easter   with a yellow splash of daffodils
end of school   the best in class

some nights   she dreams
embraced in soft arms   milky scents
then deserted   alone   up in arms

ii/

hands   her day-time asset
acquisitive of size   strength
coarse deftness

the house   farm   fields
harvests   animals   brothers
feeding   cleaning   mending

always a cygnet   never swan
father's claims growing   stunning
province of silence

out of the trail of seasons
she snatches the command
harsh like the high noon
home   church   proud bearing

grows into her savings
her small-landed security
her big shoes

Marriage

much later   different place
no online then   yet   they meet
the blue-eyed army jurist
promoted from Algeria
diligent   methodical   and she

the blue-eyed tigress
of small-town savannah
growling at 'flimflam' writing—
no ink-stained paws ever
to touch her fortune –

in the pre-nuptial   consent
of high-spirited army leave
they marry
every year he returns
in conjugal passion

once   silver bowl   snatched
waltzing on the floor
but then appeasements
intimacies   proud gestations
prompt parturitions

absent years' myths
of wedded happiness
seven years   five children
he leaves
does not return

she takes time like a heavy duster
to blackening grief
in her room's corners   her bed
scrubs it off the kitchen floor
wipes its grime off the furniture

smacks the smut on the boy's heads
           the town watches

Shadowmouth

NO
this is not happening
not to me

turning his back   slamming the door—
we have been there before
wait   look through the window
summer holiday's   coming
wait
will bring him back
look through the window   check the mail
email   1471   email   call his secretary
NO

water-mill mind
circling   wheeling   grinding
pouring
must be tears   no sound   nobody sees
night   day   night
on waking darkness falls   keeps falling
like snow   curtain of snow   blank
the last call
When things of the spirit come first
too early yet   too late already   Simone de—

call for my shots

*

why
somebody must pay

bad blood   toxic waste   hypocrisy
plenty of it around   this world   men
put them to the blade of my tongue
somebody will pay
not I

for God's sake   these are 1850's
to defy Him   upbringing   conventions
all these   our own provincial ilk
to go beyond   to surpass
my son's generation   will try   Paris will—
The Second Sex still a century to come
I will be blamed

I won't be Nobody
will not be walked over   LEFT   left-over
at thirty five I am a Widow—black dress
head held high   back straight like a sward
a swordman Widow   I am

*

but nights   ah   the nights
nights he has always had for me
love was there to be had
and he loved me

the way man loves woman

not this last summer though
the baby just born
other one toddling at my skirts
and the boys   like boys—

he was not happy
not the days   not nights
single motherhood bowl in
single-handed
missing the manly pair nightly
time of harvest

Widow Rimbaud

here comes the Widow
thirty five
she must go on
head in tight hairnet   high
like a crown

tight lips   face   buttons—
against horde's vice   sin
church lashings of eyes
market days' whispers
she will not fall

she is not for stumbling
predestined grace
hers for the taking
suffering of the chosen
balsam on her wounds

her faith
has a clock's accuracy
exactitude of judgement
no mercy   not for herself
not for them   ever

the son's matchstick sketch
black   on white
stiff ` bent   shrunk figure
hung down head—
the poet's third dimension

Mother

she fears for their salvation
life success   place in society
fatherless boys
must be taken in hand
big hand   dexterous
have never failed her yet
not before   not now

round the kitchen table
little girls are good   useful
trained to be in charge
to tell on
big brothers allowed
no deviation
from the homework

slaps   thumps   spanks
promises of extra work
supper-less bedtimes
stark home for tough children
out on the town handholding
silent two girls   two boys
scrubbed   dressed in black

memories of the poet
tokens of her care   love
marks on his head   face
his young bed's shock of pleasure
the only way she knew.

Father

father was fun
how many young boys could say that

army leave homecoming   once a year—
the gaiety would last us months

I kept examining his face
creased by the African sun—
smiling radiances
sparkles of his eyes

blue as his bleached chambray shirt
the Provencal sky   the sea
always talked about   the sky   the sea
I longed his longing

full head of blond hair   army cut
regulation moustache
bent over his notebooks
the mystery of his writing

captivated   envious
his foreign worlds   languages   manliness
jealous of neighbours   cis-het males
always gathering   applauding
how he could hold his drink   win at cards

my first day of school—last sight of the Captain
mother never forgave
his leaving us   his
happiness

Rue Bourbon

Godless place   mother mutters
good family   bad location
small income   high aspirations
street tagged with rulers' title—
its air
less of Royalty   than of cheap liquor
no extravagant aroma of Bourbon roses
no native Celtic treasures
no spring crystal waters
                              of healing sway
just ageless Celt God
in disguise of young Apollo
no lyre

                    *

to slink behind her back
watchful   proud
takes a cookie

but there he is
out of her bastion of genteel propriety
front door barred from others

into the street   the poorest end's rumpus
neighbourly familiarity
black men   grey faces   work clothes
women on doorsteps   news of the day
jokes shouted window to window
skint backyards blazing in corners
clumps of wild geranium   odd sunflower

they meet   take out their trade
his pristine lunch
for a piece of un-leavened bread
waif's mother baked on the top of stove
sliced along the edge for sprinkling of sugar
in manky hand   out of stinking trousers' pockets
offbeat delicacy

the girl next door
pounces on him   sits astride
no letting off the brat
her loose skirt over his eyes
he inhales the body's scent
bites buttocks in despair

ah to run with the sun
Easy-jetting   island hopping
to follow wanderings of father
away from childhood's dark   hardship   want
away from bourgeoisie mores   proprieties
he takes time in his hands
walks to his backyard hideout
shutting tight the door of latrine
he topples the world   plots his own

Paris

hands in my pockets
I have your cobbles under my feet
my 41 size shoes
dirty   scuffed   travelled
tied slapdash with a string
tattered coat lined with wind
my stride   vanquishing

pay attention   Paris
see
hear
stand back
I'm going to swing   into boogie

Ars Poetica
            take note
I dance across your table
snazzy rhythm   jazzy footwork
every step an idea
each turn—an invention
Number & Harmony & Torture
for I am
            the thief of fire
immigrant
from the Future
the seer

I'm coming out
City of Light
how you seduce
Celts   Bohemians   Romans
girls   geniuses   poets
in Sonia Rykiel dress
Left Bank hearts dance
Notre Dame heart cracks
while accordion wails

May 1871

neatly cut trunks of Parisian trees
piled tangle of crashed chairs   a sofa
chest hurled from the window
omnibus on its side
up-turned across the street
the silent barricade
burst   spattered
scraps of utopia wings

those were the days   cute boy
did you think they would go on?
jeered on   fouled   tobacco spat
they had you dance an ithyphallic dance
they mocked away your revolution
in slobber   blood

at the back of
his skull they keep marching
thumping boots against cobbles

slaying hands   waving flags
cocking guns   advancing
blue smoke   red fire
serving his time again and again
body retching

he stands tall
juvenile communard returns the stare
in blaze of contorted words
he blackens bridges

in slow current of suffering
takes his bath

                    *

all quiet on the narrow street
high springtime air hangs still
out of the orphaned barricade jumble
pale kitchen table sticks out
a broken limb

North East you must be walking now
my son
long way   the fields   the river
to my old kitchen table
home's true air
soft ring of candle light
your star's luminous way.

Place Vendome

cherche le père

So
how do I look in this?

the casquette   kèpi for you
peak shading my eyes the bluest blue
regulation baggy trousers   leather jambiérs
in my military stance   armed with the rifle
chasseur enough for you?

Captain Rimbaud personified
his high forehead   eyes   hair
full mouth   customised scowl of my own
not a touch of his Provencal gaiety
Shadowmouth had her searing gaze in that

be it
    she had her prison   revolution
    single mother's barricades
    all for her children   her son
be it

Is this how he looked?
taking the lead of life in ranks   such dash
foreign service   big world
writer   translator   *Qur'ân* into French
my Arabic fount

my absent father
man 'shod with wind'   the First Edition
absent   no fault   absent but not

           *

is this how he looked
how she sees him when she looks at me
as she slips out to her room
her long narrow body bent in half
like a broken leaf of the bulrush
bottle in hand   blessed Laudanum

when her hand slips under my bedcovers
when she slips in   heavy
—A son of toil just the same—

absent but not
and what is—is not
sons of men are made before the age of six
the rest is noise   contention   hurt
revolt

draining small-town place   scholars   of all there is
throwing it all   the genius   back   into their faces

presumption of goodness   in art   education
seduction

on the barricade then

28

You Happening to Me

I stretch out my hand
raindrops slide off my fingers
mermaid's hairs
liquid murmuration

I believe in rain
that it will come
more than that
I believe in sun
more than that

your thoughts and mine
like locket and clasp
my charm for
dispelling the past

trees christened anew
chiselled air
my-lady's-mantle in pearls
birds out to drink

spotty kid in baseball cap
skateboarding by
an after-splash of colour

Dear Paul

meant 2 tell you　GOK　　　　　　God only knows
U have guessed anyway
centre of me　　always　　4EVA
this terrible pain
curious　wild　searching
beyond what the world contains
something transfigured
my 'love of bad mother'
for the poor　needy　beyond pity
tears I cried
BCOZ 2 my sorrow
pain to us has grown
S2U　　　　　　　　　　same to you
centre of us 4EVER this pain
but　　listen

U know all about me
EVA hopelessly complicated
Roche only familiarity now
plain green comforts　moist scents
winds　　solid ground
vast　　under vast skyline
to connect　　to escape

U conquered ESEMED　　　　every second, every minute, every day
my silly pipe　　2 hold on 2
SLT in my assault on Paris　　something like that
my EVA knowing-it-all
U NVR laughed but with me
SWIS　　　　　　　　see what I am saying
MHOTU　　　　　　　my hat off to you

OBTW　　that summer　　oh, by the way
remember
how did we write
into autumn and winter
on and on
the best of you

30

the best of 2 of us
I NEVA thought I'll find
what I searched for
that it was 2B found
that Spirit of us EVA present

BSU   be seeing you

Dear Rimbaud

GNBLFU   got nothing but love for you
yes   let's speak of our souls
J4T   just for today
our love 4 the Spirit
reigning the world
liberated   'systematically deranged'
fire and water   earth and wind
in unity

our Ars Poetica
we R set free
unbound
no vain Eloquence   no Rhyme
words   now right   now wrong
WNOHGB   where no one has gone before

?4U   have a question for you
H/C UR sudden departure   how come your
and now I cannot write
CRBT   crying real big tears
CRB   come right back
come down to Tuileries
all your green scents
come back
GNBLFU

31

Mad at You

In a grip of
darkness
music's last breath
expires

Red Fury is back
her entourage
in full attendance
visitations of terror

when she sings
nothing is over
when she goes
she stays

curl of the lip
lingering
obliterating   blotting out
the remainder of us

The Woman of Harare

that first day
burst upon us
sunburnt   red-ripe
heavy with fruit
on mulberry bushes

I watch
your searching fingers
tender   insistent
amongst the leaves
all secret places

your hands
cupped around berries
sharing the harvest
sweet rills of noontide
flowing   dripping

Eurydice
sister of migrating moon
in the dawning of light
your bronze arms glow
the sand-dune shimmer

at a niche of your body
desert seashell hum
we are drowning
I am drowning
in song of the sun

Epilogue

you come to me long after
past scaring sun   burning sand
cancer torture   the butchered leg

past killing fields of the Great War
your soldier boots bloodied
with the scraps of the century

father   grandfather
heart of child reconciled
hands touching   mouth kissing

beauty of milky stars Golden Way
joyous Astarte   all year offerings
summer ways

it has been found—

eternity

UK Ltd.

/286